STEP-BY-STEP

Indian Vegetarian Cooking

STEP-BY-STEP

Indian Vegetarian Cooking

LOUISE STEELE

||| •PARRAGON• |||

First published in Great Britain in 1994 by
Parragon Book Service Ltd
Unit 13–17
Avonbridge Trading Estate
Atlantic Road
Avonmouth
Bristol BS11 9QD

ISBN 1-85813-629-6 (hbk)
ISBN 0-75251-208-0 (pbk)

Printed in Italy

Acknowledgements:
Design & DTP: Pedro & Frances Prá-Lopez/Kingfisher Design
Art Direction: Clive Hayball
Managing Editor: Alexa Stace
Special Photography: Martin Brigdale
Home Economist: Jill Eggleton
Step-by-step Photography: Karl Adamson
Step-by-step Home Economist: Joanna Craig
Styling: Helen Trent

Gas hob supplied by New World Domestic Appliances Ltd.

Photographs on pages 6, 18, 26, 56 and 66 reproduced by permission of
Tony Stone Images.

Note:
Cup measurements in this book are for American cups. Tablespoons are assumed to be 15 ml.
Unless otherwise stated, milk is assumed to be full-fat, eggs are standard size 2 and pepper is freshly
ground black pepper.

Contents

SOUPS & STARTERS *page* 7

Indian Bean Soup.............................8
Minted Pea & Yogurt Soup 11
Spicy Dal & Carrot Soup......................12
Spiced Corn & Nut Mix 14
Garlicky Mushroom Pakoras 16
Vegetable & Cashew Samosas 19

MAIN DISHES *page* 21

Egg & Lentil Curry............................22
Brown Rice with Fruit & Nuts 24
Muttar Paneer 27
Split Peas with Vegetables 28
Stuffed Aubergine (Eggplant) 31
Lentil & Vegetable Biriyani 32
Jacket Potatoes with Beans.................34
Spinach & Aubergine (Eggplant) 36
Vegetable Nut & Lentil Koftas 38
Chick-Peas & Aubergines (Eggplant) 41
Vegetable Curry 42
Spiced Basmati Pilau.........................44

ACCOMPANIMENTS *page* 47

Curried Okra 48
Aubergine (Eggplant) in Saffron 51
Spinach & Cauliflower Bhaji 52
Fried Spiced Potatoes 55
Mixed (Bell) Pepper Pooris 56
Sweet Hot Carrots & Beans 58
Potato Fritters with Relish 61
Parathas 63

DESSERTS *page* 65

Mango Ice-cream 66
Saffron-spiced Rice Pudding 69
Coconut Cream Moulds 70
Sweet Carrot Halva..........................73

INDIAN VEGETARIAN COOKING *page* 74

Spices 74
Accompaniments..............................74
Drinks 76
Storecupboard Standbys 76
Pulses 78

Index 80

CHAPTER ONE

Soups & Starters

If a dessert is the crowning grand finale to a meal then a starter must be the opening overture, and should be orchestrated to tease the tastebuds and tempt the appetite. The repertoire of vegetarian Indian dishes to fulfil this role are fortunately wide and varied. Soups are a natural choice for the prepare-ahead cook and can be made thick and hearty with pulses like beans and lentils to satisfy large appetites. Some soups, like Indian Bean Soup and Spicy Dal and Carrot Soup will also double up beautifully as light lunch dishes. Others provide a lighter, more refreshing start, as in Minted Pea and Yogurt Soup.

In India, starters are rarely served as such, and would instead accompany a meal. These typical dishes do, however, fill the role of appetizers and are just perfect to serve with drinks at informal buffet parties. Vegetable and Nut Samosas and Garlicky Mushroom Pakoras can be made well ahead and reheated before serving, and Spiced Corn and Nut Mix makes a superb alternative to the predictable peanut and crisp offerings with drinks.

Opposite: *Transporting supplies by canoe in Kerala.*

STEP 1

STEP 2

STEP 3

STEP 4

INDIAN BEAN SOUP

A thick and hearty soup, nourishing and substantial enough to serve as a main meal with wholemeal bread. Black-eye beans are used here, but red kidney beans or chick-peas may be added to the mixture if preferred.

SERVES 4-6

4 tbsp ghee or vegetable oil
2 onions, peeled and chopped
250 g/8 oz/1½ cups potato, peeled and cut
  into chunks
250 g/8 oz/1½ cups parsnip, peeled and cut
  into chunks
250 g/8 oz/1½ cups turnip or swede, peeled
  and cut into chunks
2 celery sticks, trimmed and sliced
2 courgettes (zucchini), trimmed and sliced
1 green (bell) pepper, seeded and cut into
  1 cm/½ inch pieces
2 garlic cloves, peeled and crushed
2 tsp ground coriander
1 tbsp paprika
1 tbsp mild curry paste
1.25 litres/2 pints/5 cups vegetable stock
salt
1 x 475 g/15 oz can black-eye beans,
  drained and rinsed
chopped fresh coriander, to garnish
  (optional)

1 Heat the ghee or oil in a saucepan, add all the prepared vegetables, except the courgettes (zucchini) and green (bell) pepper, and cook over a moderate heat for 5 minutes, stirring frequently. Add the garlic, coriander, paprika and curry paste and cook for 1 minute, stirring.

2 Stir in the stock and season with salt to taste. Bring to the boil, cover and simmer gently for 25 minutes, stirring occasionally.

3 Stir in the beans, sliced courgettes (zucchini) and green (bell) pepper, cover and continue cooking for a further 15 minutes or until all the vegetables are tender.

4 Purée 300 ml/½ pint/1¼ cups of the soup mixture (about 2 ladlefuls) in a food processor or blender. Return the puréed mixture to the soup in the saucepan and reheat until piping hot. Sprinkle with chopped coriander, if using and serve hot.

COOK'S TIPS

For a thinner, broth-type consistency to the soup, do not purée the two ladlefuls of mixture as instructed at step 4. The flavour of this soup improves if made the day before it is required, as this allows time for all the flavours to blend and develop.

MINTED PEA & YOGURT SOUP

A deliciously refreshing soup that is full of goodness. It is also extremely tasty served chilled – in which case you may like to thin the consistency a little more with extra stock, yogurt or milk, as wished.

STEP 1

SERVES 6

2 tbsp vegetable ghee or oil
2 onions, peeled and coarsely chopped
250 g/8 oz potato, peeled and coarsely chopped
2 garlic cloves, peeled
2.5 cm/1 inch ginger root, peeled and chopped
1 tsp ground coriander
1 tsp ground cumin
1 tbsp plain flour
900 ml/1 1/2 pints/3 1/2 cups vegetable stock
500 g/1 lb frozen peas
2-3 tbsp chopped fresh mint, to taste
salt and freshly ground black pepper
150 ml/1/4 pint/2/3 cup strained Greek yogurt
1/2 tsp cornflour (cornstarch)
300 ml/1/2 pint/1 1/4 cups milk
a little extra yogurt, for serving (optional)
mint sprigs, to garnish

1 Heat the ghee or oil in a saucepan, add the onions and potato and cook gently for 3 minutes. Stir in the garlic, ginger, coriander, cumin and flour and cook for 1 minute, stirring.

2 Add the stock, peas and half the mint and bring to the boil, stirring. Reduce the heat, cover and simmer gently for 15 minutes or until the vegetables are tender.

STEP 2

3 Purée the soup, in batches, in a blender or food processor. Return the mixture to the pan and season with salt and pepper to taste. Blend the yogurt with the cornflour (cornstarch) and stir into the soup.

4 Add the milk and bring almost to the boil, stirring all the time. Cook very gently for 2 minutes. Serve hot, sprinkled with the remaining mint and a swirl of extra yogurt, if wished.

STEP 3a

COOK'S TIP

The yogurt is mixed with a little cornflour (cornstarch) before being added to the hot soup – this helps to stabilize the yogurt and prevents it separating when heated.

STEP 3b

STEP 1

STEP 2

STEP 3

STEP 4

SPICY DAL & CARROT SOUP

This delicious, warming and nutritious soup uses split red lentils and carrots as the two main ingredients and includes a selection of spices to give it a "kick". It is simple to make and extremely good to eat.

SERVES 6

125 g/4 oz split red lentils
1.25 litres/2 pints/5 cups vegetable stock
350 g/12 oz carrots, peeled and sliced
2 onions, peeled and chopped
1 x 250 g/8 oz can chopped tomatoes
2 garlic cloves, peeled and chopped
2 tbsp vegetable ghee or oil
1 tsp ground cumin
1 tsp ground coriander
1 fresh green chilli, seeded and chopped, or
    use 1 tsp minced chilli (from a jar)
½ tsp ground turmeric
15 ml/1 tbsp lemon juice
salt
300 ml/½ pint/1¼ cups milk
30 ml/2 tbsp chopped fresh coriander
yogurt, to serve

1 Place the lentils in a sieve and wash well under cold running water. Drain and place in a large saucepan with 900 ml/1½ pints/3½ cups of the stock, the carrots, onions, tomatoes and garlic. Bring the mixture to the boil, reduce the heat, cover and simmer for 30 minutes or until the vegetables and lentils are tender.

2 Meanwhile, heat the ghee or oil in a small pan, add the cumin,

coriander, chilli and turmeric and fry gently for 1 minute. Remove from the heat and stir in the lemon juice and salt to taste.

3 Purée the soup in batches in a blender or food processor. Return the soup to the saucepan, add the spice mixture and the remaining 300 ml/½ pint/1¼ cups stock or water and simmer for 10 minutes.

4 Add the milk, taste and adjust the seasoning, if necessary. Stir in the chopped coriander and reheat gently. Serve hot, with a swirl of yogurt.

VARIATION

As this soup has quite a hot and spicy flavour, it may be wise to omit or at least reduce the amount of chilli in the recipe when serving it to children. A spoonful of natural yogurt, swirled into each serving of soup makes it extra nutritious and delicious.

STEP 1a

STEP 2

STEP 3

STEP 4

SPICED CORN & NUT MIX

A tasty mixture of buttery-spiced nuts, raisins and popcorn to enjoy as a snack or with pre-dinner drinks.

SERVES 6

2 tbsp vegetable oil
60 g/2 oz/¼ cup popping corn
60 g/2 oz/¼ cup butter
1 garlic clove, peeled and crushed
60 g/2 oz/⅓ cup unblanched almonds
60 g/2 oz/½ cup unsalted cashews
60 g/2 oz /1½ cup unsalted peanuts
1 tsp Worcestershire sauce
1 tsp curry powder or paste
¼ tsp chilli powder
60 g/2 oz/⅓ cup seedless raisins
salt

1 Heat the oil in a saucepan. Add the popping corn, stir well, then cover and cook over a fairly high heat for 3-5 minutes, holding the saucepan lid firmly and shaking the pan frequently until the popping stops.

2 Turn the popped corn into a dish, discarding any unpopped corn kernels.

3 Melt the butter in a frying pan, add the garlic, almonds, cashews and peanuts, then stir in the Worcestershire sauce, curry powder or paste and chilli powder and cook over medium heat for 2-3 minutes, stirring frequently.

4 Remove the pan from the heat and stir in the raisins and popped corn. Season with salt to taste and mix well. Transfer to a serving bowl and serve warm or cold.

VARIATIONS

Use a mixture of any unsalted nuts of your choice – walnuts, pecans, hazelnuts, Brazils, macadamia nuts and pine kernels are all delicious prepared this way. For a less fiery flavour omit the curry powder and chilli powder and add instead 1 tsp cumin seeds, 1 tsp ground coriander and ½ tsp paprika. Sprinkle with 1-2 tbsp of chopped fresh coriander just before serving.

STEP 1

STEP 2

STEP 3

STEP 4

GARLICKY MUSHROOM PAKORAS

*Whole mushrooms are dunked in a spiced garlicky batter and
deep fried until golden. They are at their most delicious
served hot and freshly cooked.*

SERVES 6

175 g/6 oz/1½ cups gram flour
½ tsp salt
¼ tsp baking powder
1 tsp cumin seeds
½-1 tsp chilli powder, to taste
200 ml/7 fl oz/¾ cup water
2 garlic cloves, peeled and crushed
1 small onion, peeled and finely chopped
vegetable oil, for deep frying
500 g/1 lb button mushrooms, trimmed
   and wiped
lemon wedges and coriander sprigs, to
   garnish

1 Put the gram flour, salt, baking powder, cumin and chilli powder into a bowl and mix well together. Make a well in the centre of the mixture and gradually stir in the water, mixing to form a batter.

2 Stir the crushed garlic and the chopped onion into the batter and leave the mixture to infuse for 10 minutes. One-third fill a deep-fat fryer or pan with vegetable oil and heat to 180°C/350°F or until hot enough to brown a cube of day-old bread in 30 seconds. Lower the basket into the hot oil.

3 Meanwhile, mix the mushrooms into the batter, stirring to coat. Remove a few at a time and place them into the hot oil. Fry for about 2 minutes or until golden brown.

4 Remove from the pan with a slotted spoon and drain on paper towels while cooking the remainder in the same way. Serve hot, sprinkled with coarse salt and garnished with lemon wedges and coriander sprigs.

GRAM FLOUR

Gram flour (also known as besan flour) is a pale yellow flour made from chick peas. It is now readily available from larger supermarkets as well as Indian food shops and some ethnic delicatessens. Gram flour is also used to make onion bhajis.

VEGETABLE & CASHEW SAMOSAS

These delicious little fried pastries are really quite simple to make.
Serve them hot as a starter to an Indian meal or cold as
a tasty picnic or lunch-box snack.

STEP 1

MAKES 12

350 g/12 oz potatoes, peeled and diced
salt
125 g/4 oz frozen peas
45 ml/3 tbsp vegetable oil
1 onion, peeled and chopped
2.5 cm/1 in ginger root, peeled and chopped
1 garlic clove, peeled and crushed
1 tsp garam masala
2 tsp mild curry paste
½ tsp cumin seeds
2 tsp lemon juice
60 g/2 oz/½ cup unsalted cashews,
    coarsely chopped
vegetable oil, for shallow frying
coriander sprigs, to garnish
mango chutney, to serve

PASTRY:
250 g/8 oz/2 cups plain flour
60 g/2 oz/¼ cup butter
75 ml/6 tbsp/⅓ cup warm milk

1 Cook the potatoes in a saucepan of boiling, salted water for 5 minutes. Add the peas and cook for a further 4 minutes or until the potato is tender. Drain well. Heat the oil in a frying pan, add the onion, potato and pea mixture, ginger, garlic and spices and fry for 2 minutes. Stir in the lemon juice and cook

STEP 2

gently, uncovered, for 2 minutes. Remove from the heat, slightly mash the potato and peas, then add the cashews, mix well and season with salt.

2 To make the pastry, put the flour in a bowl and rub in the butter finely. Mix in the milk to form a dough. Knead lightly and divide into 6 portions. Form each into a ball and roll out on a lightly floured surface to an 18 cm/7 inch round. Cut each one in half.

3 Divide the filling equally between each semi-circle of pastry, spreading it out to within 5 mm/¼ in of the edges. Brush the edges of pastry all the way round with water and fold over to form triangular shapes, sealing the edges well together to enclose the filling completely.

STEP 3

4 One-third fill a large, deep frying pan with oil and heat to 180°C/350°F/Gas 4 or until hot enough to brown a cube of bread in 30 seconds. Fry the samosas, a few at a time, turning frequently until golden brown and heated through. Drain on papertowels and keep warm while cooking the remainder in the same way. Garnish with coriander sprigs and serve hot.

STEP 4

CHAPTER TWO

Main Dishes

India has long stood as the undisputed centre of vegetarianism. This is partly due to religious reasons (Hindus are forbidden meat), and partly due to economic factors. The vegetarian dishes they eat therefore supply all the proteins, vitamins and minerals that the human body needs.

The Indians make great use and show creative flair in using their staples of rice, lentils, fruit, nuts, eggs, milk, pulses and vegetables to make a seemingly endless array of dishes from biryanis and curries to pilaus and paneers that delight the appetite.

Such basic foodstuffs are used to create spicy, wholesome curries; stuffed vegetable treats using aubergines and potatoes; rice and vegetable pilaus with crunchy nut crowns; and nut and lentil "meatballs" better known as koftas. Mixed and matched with flavoursome rice, lentil, vegetable and bread accompaniments, they make a nutritious feast for the vegetarian.

Opposite: *Ploughing a rice paddy with the help of water buffaloes, near Madras.*

STEP 1

STEP 2

STEP 3

STEP 4

EGG & LENTIL CURRY

A nutritious meal that is easy and relatively quick to make. The curried lentil sauce would also be delicious served with cooked vegetables such as cauliflower, potato and aubergine (eggplant).

SERVES 4

3 tbsp vegetable ghee or oil
1 large onion, peeled and chopped
2 garlic cloves, peeled and chopped
2.5 cm/ 1 in ginger root, peeled and
   chopped
1/2 tsp minced chilli (from a jar), or use
   chilli powder
1 tsp ground coriander
1 tsp ground cumin
1 tsp paprika
90 g/ 3 oz split red lentils
450 ml / 3/4 pint/ 1 3/4 cups vegetable stock
1 x 250 g/ 8 oz can chopped tomatoes
6 eggs
50 ml/ 2 fl oz/ 1/4 cup coconut milk
salt
2 tomatoes, cut into wedges, and coriander
   sprigs, to garnish
parathas, chapatis or naan bread, to serve

1 Heat the ghee or oil in a saucepan, add the onion and fry gently for 3 minutes. Stir in the garlic, ginger, chilli and spices and cook gently for 1 minute, stirring frequently. Stir in the lentils, stock and chopped tomatoes and bring to the boil. Reduce the heat, cover and simmer gently for 30 minutes, stirring occasionally until the lentils and onion are tender.

2 Meanwhile, place the eggs in a saucepan of cold water and bring to the boil. Reduce the heat and simmer for 10 minutes. Drain and cover immediately with cold water.

3 Stir the coconut milk into the lentil mixture and season well with salt to taste. Purée the mixture in a blender or food processor until smooth. Return to the pan and heat through.

4 Shell and cut the hard-boiled eggs in half lengthways. Arrange 3 halves, in a petal design, on each serving plate. Spoon the hot lentil sauce over the eggs, adding enough to flood the serving plate. Arrange a tomato wedge and a coriander sprig between each halved egg. Serve hot with parathas, chapatis or naan bread to mop up the sauce.

COOK'S NOTE

Eggs contain high quality protein, fat, iron, and Vitamins A, D and B, although they are also high in cholesterol. Incidentally, a brown-shelled egg and a rich yellow yolk makes no difference to the food value.

STEP 1

STEP 2

STEP 3

STEP 4

BROWN RICE WITH FRUIT & NUTS

Here is a tasty and filling rice dish that is nice and spicy and includes fruits for a refreshing flavour and toasted nuts for an interesting crunchy texture.

SERVES 4-6

4 tbsp vegetable ghee or oil
1 large onion, peeled and chopped
2 garlic cloves, peeled and crushed
2.5 cm/ 1 in ginger root, peeled and chopped
1 tsp chilli powder
1 tsp cumin seeds
1 tbsp mild or medium curry powder or paste
300 g/ 10 oz/ 1 1/2 cups brown rice
900 ml/ 1 1/2 pints/ 3 1/2 cups boiling vegetable stock
1 x 425 g/ 14 oz can chopped tomatoes
salt and freshly ground black pepper
175 g/ 6 oz ready-soaked dried apricots or peaches, cut into slivers
1 red (bell) pepper, cored, seeded and diced
90 g/ 3 oz frozen peas
1-2 small, slightly green bananas
60-90g/ 2-3 oz/ 1/3-1/2 cup toasted nuts (a mixture of almonds, cashews and hazelnuts, or pine kernels)
coriander sprigs, to garnish

1 Heat the ghee or oil in a large saucepan, add the onion and fry gently for 3 minutes. Stir in the garlic, ginger, spices and rice and cook gently for 2 minutes, stirring all the time until the rice is coated in the spiced oil.

2 Pour in the boiling stock and add the canned tomatoes and season with salt and pepper to taste. Bring to the boil, then reduce the heat, cover and simmer gently for 40 minutes or until the rice is almost cooked and most of the liquid is absorbed.

3 Add the slivered apricots or peaches, diced red (bell) pepper and peas. Cover and continue cooking for 10 minutes. Remove from the heat and allow to stand for 5 minutes without uncovering.

4 Peel and slice the bananas. Uncover the rice mixture and fork through to mix the ingredients together. Add the toasted nuts and sliced banana and toss lightly. Transfer to a warm serving platter and garnish with coriander sprigs. Serve hot.

COOK'S NOTE

Brown rice has a delicious nutty flavour and a more chewy texture than white rice and because the germ of the grain is retained, it also contains larger amounts of vitamins, minerals and protein. Brown rice takes longer to cook than white rice.

MUTTAR PANEER

Paneer is a delicious fresh, soft cheese frequently used in Indian cooking. It is easily made at home, but remember to make it the day before required.

STEP 1

SERVES 6

150 ml/¹/₄ pint/²/₃ cup vegetable oil
2 onions, peeled and chopped
2 garlic cloves, peeled and crushed
2.5 cm/1 in ginger root, peeled and chopped
1 tsp garam masala
1 tsp ground turmeric
1 tsp chilli powder
500 g/1 lb frozen peas
1 x 250 g/8 oz can chopped tomatoes
125 ml/4 fl oz/¹/₂ cup vegetable stock
salt and freshly ground black pepper
2 tbsp chopped fresh coriander

PANEER:

2.5 litres/4 pints/10 cups pasteurized full cream milk
5 tbsp lemon juice
1 garlic clove, peeled and crushed (optional)
1 tbsp chopped fresh coriander (optional)

1 Bring the milk to a rolling boil in a large saucepan. Remove from the heat and stir in the lemon juice. Return to the heat for about 1 minute until the curds and whey separate. Remove from the heat. Line a colander with double thickness muslin and pour the mixture through the muslin, adding the garlic and coriander, if using. Squeeze all the liquid from the curds and leave to drain.

2 Transfer to a dish, cover with a plate and weights and leave overnight in the refrigerator.

3 Cut the pressed paneer into small cubes. Heat the oil in a large frying pan, add the paneer cubes and fry until golden on all sides. Remove from the pan and drain on paper towels.

4 Pour off some of the oil, leaving about 4 tablespoons in the pan. Add the onions, garlic and ginger and fry gently for about 5 minutes, stirring frequently. Stir in the spices and fry gently for 2 minutes. Add the peas, tomatoes and stock and season with salt and pepper. Cover and simmer for 10 minutes, stirring occasionally, until the onion is tender. Add the fried paneer cubes and cook for a further 5 minutes. Taste and adjust the seasoning, if necessary. Sprinkle with the coriander and serve at once.

STEP 3

STEP 4a

STEP 4b

STEP 2

STEP 3

STEP 4

STEP 5

SPLIT PEAS WITH VEGETABLES

Here is a simple, yet nourishing and flavourful way of cooking yellow split peas. Vary the selection of vegetables and spices according to personal preferences.

SERVES 4-5

250 g/8 oz/1 cup dried yellow split peas
1.25 litres/2 pints/5 cups cold water
¹/₂ tsp ground turmeric (optional)
500g/1 lb new potatoes, scrubbed
75 ml/5 tbsp/¹/₃ cup vegetable oil
2 onions, peeled and coarsely chopped
175 g/6 oz button mushrooms, wiped
1 tsp ground coriander
1 tsp ground cumin
1 tsp chilli powder
1 tsp garam masala
salt and freshly ground black pepper
450 ml/³/₄ pint/1³/₄ cups vegetable stock
¹/₂ cauliflower, broken into florets
90 g/3 oz frozen peas
175 g/6 oz cherry tomatoes and halved
  mint sprigs, to garnish

1 Place the split peas in a bowl, add the cold water and leave to soak for at least 4 hours or overnight.

2 Place the peas and the soaking liquid in a fairly large saucepan, stir in the turmeric, if using, and bring to the boil. Skim off any surface scum, half-cover the pan with a lid and simmer gently for 20 minutes or until the peas are tender and almost dry. Remove the pan from the heat and reserve.

3 Meanwhile, cut the potatoes into 5 mm (¼ inch) thick slices. Heat the oil in a flameproof casserole, add the onions, potatoes and mushrooms and cook gently for 5 minutes, stirring frequently. Stir in the spices and fry gently for 1 minute, then add salt and pepper to taste, stock and cauliflower florets.

4 Cover and simmer gently for 25 minutes or until the potato is tender, stirring occasionally. Add the split peas (and any of the cooking liquid) and the frozen peas. Bring to the boil, cover and continue cooking for 5 minutes.

5 Stir in the halved cherry tomatoes and cook for 2 minutes. Taste and adjust the seasoning, if necessary. Serve hot, garnished with mint sprigs.

VARIATION

Chana dal (popular with vegetarians because of its high protein content) may be used instead of yellow split peas, if preferred. Chana dal is similar to yellow split peas, although the grains are smaller and the flavour sweeter.

STUFFED AUBERGINES (EGGPLANT)

These are delicious served hot or cold, topped with natural yogurt or cucumber raita.

STEP 1

SERVES 6

OVEN: 180°C / 350°F / GAS 4

250 g / 8 oz / 1⅓ cup continental lentils
900 ml / 1½ pints / 3¾ cups water
2 garlic cloves, peeled and crushed
3 well-shaped aubergines (eggplants), leaf ends trimmed
150 ml / ¼ pint / ⅔ cup vegetable oil
salt and freshly ground black pepper
2 onions, peeled and chopped
4 tomatoes, chopped
2 tsp cumin seeds
1 tsp ground cinnamon
2 tbsp mild curry paste
1 tsp minced chilli (from a jar)
2 tbsp chopped fresh mint
natural yogurt and mint sprigs, to serve

1 Rinse the lentils under cold running water. Drain and place in a saucepan with the water and garlic. Cover and simmer for 30 minutes.

2 Cook the aubergines (eggplants) in a saucepan of boiling water for 5 minutes. Drain, then plunge into cold water for 5 minutes. Drain again, then cut the aubergines (eggplants) in half lengthways and scoop out most of the flesh and reserve, leaving a 1 cm / ½ in thick border to form a shell.

3 Place the aubergine (eggplant) shells in a shallow greased ovenproof dish, brush with a little oil and sprinkle with salt and pepper. Cook in the preheated oven for 10 minutes. Meanwhile, heat half the remaining oil in a frying pan, add the onions and tomatoes and fry gently for 5 minutes. Chop the reserved aubergine (eggplant) flesh, add to the pan with the spices and cook gently for 5 minutes. Season with salt.

4 Stir in the lentils, most of the remaining oil, reserving a little for later, and the mint. Spoon the mixture into the shells. Drizzle with remaining oil and bake for 15 minutes. Serve hot or cold topped with a spoonful of natural yogurt and mint sprigs.

STEP 2

STEP 3

COOK'S TIP

Choose nice plump aubergines (eggplant) rather than thin tapering ones as these retain their shape better when filled and baked with a stuffing.

STEP 4

STEP 1a

STEP 1b

STEP 2

STEP 3

LENTIL & VEGETABLE BIRYANI

A delicious mix of vegetables, basmati rice and continental lentils produces a wholesome and nutritious dish.

SERVES 6

125 g/4 oz/²/₃ cup continental lentils
4 tbsp vegetable ghee or oil
2 onions, peeled, quartered and sliced
2 garlic cloves, peeled and crushed
2.5 cm/1 in ginger root, peeled and chopped
1 tsp ground turmeric
¹/₂ tsp chilli powder
1 tsp ground coriander
2 tsp ground cumin
3 tomatoes, skinned and chopped
1 aubergine (eggplant), trimmed and cut in
    1 cm/¹/₂ in pieces
1.75 litres/2¹/₂ pints/6¹/₄ cups boiling
    vegetable stock
1 red or green (bell) pepper, cored, seeded
    and diced
350 g/12 oz/1³/₄ cups basmati rice
125 g/4 oz/1 cup French beans, topped,
    tailed and halved
250 g/8 oz/1¹/₃ cups cauliflower florets
125 g/4 oz/1¹/₂ mushrooms, wiped and
    sliced or quartered
60 g/2 oz/¹/₂ cup unsalted cashews
3 hard-boiled eggs, shelled, to garnish
coriander sprigs, to garnish

1 Rinse the lentils under cold running water and drain. Heat the ghee or oil in a saucepan, add the onions and fry gently for 2 minutes. Stir in the garlic, ginger and spices and fry gently for 1 minute, stirring frequently. Add the lentils, tomatoes, aubergine (eggplant) and 600 ml/1 pint/2½ cups of the stock, mix well, then cover and simmer gently for 20 minutes. Add the red or green (bell) pepper and cook for a further 10 minutes or until the lentils are tender and all the liquid has been absorbed.

2 Meanwhile, place the rice in a sieve and rinse under cold running water until the water runs clear. Drain and place in another pan with the remaining stock. Bring to the boil, add the French beans, cauliflower and mushrooms, then cover and cook gently for 15 minutes or until rice and vegetables are tender. Remove from the heat and leave, covered, for 10 minutes.

3 Add the lentil mixture and the cashews to the cooked rice and mix lightly together. Pile onto a warm serving platter and garnish with wedges of hard-boiled egg and coriander sprigs. Serve hot.

STEP 1

STEP 2

STEP 3a

STEP 3b

JACKET POTATOES WITH BEANS

Baked jacket potatoes, topped with a tasty mixture of beans in a spicy sauce, provide a deliciously filling, high-fibre dish.

SERVES 6
OVEN: 200°C/400°F/GAS 6

6 large potatoes (for baking)
4 tbsp vegetable ghee or oil
1 large onion, peeled and chopped
2 garlic cloves, peeled and crushed
1 tsp ground turmeric
1 tbsp cumin seeds
2 tbsp mild or medium curry paste
350 g/12 oz cherry tomatoes
1 x 425 g/14 oz can black-eye beans, drained and rinsed
1 x 425 g/14 oz can red kidney beans, drained and rinsed
1 tbsp lemon juice
2 tbsp tomato purée (paste)
150 ml/¼ pint/⅔ cup water
2 tbsp chopped fresh mint or coriander
salt and freshly ground black pepper
natural yogurt, to serve
mint sprigs, to garnish

1 Wash and scrub the potatoes and prick several times with a fork. Place in the oven and cook for 1-1¼ hours or until the potatoes feel soft when gently squeezed.

2 About 20 minutes before the end of cooking time, prepare the topping. Heat the ghee or oil in a saucepan, add the onion and cook gently for 5 minutes, stirring frequently. Add the garlic, turmeric, cumin seeds and curry paste and cook gently for 1 minute. Stir in the tomatoes, black-eye beans and red kidney beans, lemon juice, tomato purée (paste), water and chopped mint. Season with salt and pepper, then cover and cook gently for 10 minutes, stirring frequently.

3 When the potatoes are cooked, cut them in half and mash the flesh lightly with a fork. Spoon the prepared bean mixture on top, garnish with mint or coriander sprigs and serve with a dish of natural yogurt.

VARIATION

Instead of cutting the potatoes in half, cut a cross in each and squeeze gently to open out. Spoon some of the prepared filling into the cross and place any remaining filling to the side.

STEP 1

STEP 2

STEP 3

STEP 3b

SPINACH & AUBERGINE (EGGPLANT)

This interesting combination of lentils and spiced vegetables is delicious served with parathas, chapatis or naan bread, plus a bowl of natural yogurt.

SERVES 4

250 g/ 8 oz/ 1 cup split red lentils
750 ml/ 1¼ pints/ 3 cups water
1 onion
1 aubergine (eggplant)
1 red (bell) pepper
2 courgettes (zucchini)
125 g/ 4 oz mushrooms, wiped
250 g/ 8 oz leaf spinach
4 tbsp vegetable ghee or oil
1 fresh green chilli, seeded and chopped, or
  use 1 tsp minced chilli (from a jar)
1 tsp ground cumin
1 tsp ground coriander
2.5 cm/ 1 in ginger root, peeled and chopped
150 ml/¼ pint/⅔ cup vegetable stock
salt
coriander or flat-leaved parsley sprigs, to
  garnish

1 Wash the lentils and place in a saucepan with the water. Cover and simmer for 15 minutes until the lentils are soft but still whole.

2 Meanwhile, peel, quarter and slice the onion. Trim leaf end and cut the aubergine (eggplant) into 1 cm /½ in pieces. Remove stalk end and seeds from the (bell) pepper and cut into 1 cm/½ in pieces. Trim and cut courgettes (zucchini) into 1 cm/½ in thick slices. Thickly slice the mushrooms. Discard coarse stalks from spinach leaves and wash spinach well.

3 Heat the ghee or oil in a large saucepan, add the onion and red (bell) pepper and fry gently for 3 minutes, stirring frequently. Stir in the aubergine (eggplant), mushrooms, chilli, spices and ginger and fry gently for 1 minute. Add the spinach and stock and season with salt to taste. Stir and turn until the spinach leaves wilt down. Cover and simmer for 10 minutes or until the vegetables are just tender.

4 Make a border of the lentils on a warm serving plate and spoon the vegetable mixture into the centre. (The lentils may be stirred into the vegetable mixture, instead of being used as a border, if wished.) Garnish with coriander or flat-leaved parsley sprigs.

SPINACH

Wash the spinach thoroughly in several changes of cold water as it can be gritty. Drain well and shake off excess water from leaves before adding to the pan.

STEP 2

STEP 3

STEP 4

STEP 5

VEGETABLE, NUT & LENTIL KOFTAS

The mixture here is shaped into golf-ball shapes and baked in the oven with a sprinkling of aromatic garam masala. Delicious served hot (or cold) with a yogurt dressing and chapatis.

SERVES 4-5
OVEN: 180°C/350°F/GAS 4

6 tbsp vegetable ghee or oil
1 onion, peeled and finely chopped
2 carrots, peeled and finely chopped
2 celery sticks, trimmed and finely chopped
2 garlic cloves, peeled and crushed
1 fresh green chilli, seeded and finely
    chopped
1½ tbsp curry powder or paste
250 g/8 oz/1¼ cups split red lentils
600 ml/1 pint/2½ cups vegetable stock
30 ml/2 tbsp tomato purée (paste)
125 g/4 oz/2 cups fresh wholewheat
    breadcrumbs
90 g/3 oz/¾ cup unsalted cashews, finely
    chopped
2 tbsp chopped fresh coriander or parsley
1 egg, beaten
salt and freshly ground black pepper
garam masala, for sprinkling

YOGURT DRESSING:
250 g/8 oz natural yogurt
1-2 tbsp chopped fresh coriander or parsley
1-2 tbsp mango chutney, chopped if
    necessary

1 Heat 4 tablespoons of ghee or oil in a large saucepan and gently fry the onion, carrots, celery, garlic and chilli for 5 minutes, stirring frequently. Add the curry powder or paste and the lentils and cook gently for 1 minute, stirring.

2 Add the stock and tomato purée (paste) and bring to the boil. Reduce the heat, cover and simmer for 20 minutes or until the lentils are tender and all the liquid is absorbed.

3 Remove from the heat and cool slightly. Add the breadcrumbs, nuts, coriander, egg and seasoning to taste. Mix well and leave to cool. Shape into rounds about the size of golf balls (the mixture is quite soft, so use 2 spoons to help shape the rounds, if necessary).

4 Place the balls on a greased baking sheet, drizzle with the remaining oil and sprinkle with a little garam masala, to taste. Cook in the preheated oven for 15-20 minutes or until piping hot and lightly golden.

5 Meanwhile, make the yogurt dressing. Mix all the ingredients together in a bowl. Serve the koftas hot with the yogurt dressing.

CHICK-PEAS & AUBERGINE (EGGPLANT)

*Canned chick-peas (widely available from supermarkets) are used in
this dish, but you could use black-eye beans or red kidney beans
if you prefer. Omit the chillies for a less fiery flavour.*

STEP 1a

SERVES 4

1 large aubergine (eggplant)
2 courgettes (zucchini)
6 tbsp vegetable ghee or oil
1 large onion, peeled, quartered and sliced
2 garlic cloves, peeled and crushed
1-2 fresh green chillies, seeded and chopped,
    or use 1-2 tsp minced chilli (from a jar)
2 tsp ground coriander
2 tsp cumin seeds
1 tsp ground turmeric
1 tsp garam masala
1 x 425 g/14 oz can chopped tomatoes
300 ml/$^{1}/_{2}$ pint/ 1$^{1}/_{4}$ cups vegetable stock or
    water
salt and freshly ground black pepper
1 x 425 g/14 oz can chick-peas, drained and
    rinsed
2 tbsp chopped fresh mint
150 ml/$^{1}/_{4}$ pint/$^{2}/_{3}$ cup double (heavy)
    cream

1 Trim the leaf end off aubergine
(eggplant) and cut into cubes. Trim
and slice the courgettes (zucchini). Heat
the ghee or oil in a saucepan and gently
fry the aubergine (eggplant), courgettes
(zucchini), onion, garlic and chillies for
about 5 minutes, stirring frequently and
adding a little more oil to the pan, if
necessary.

2 Stir in the spices and cook for 30
seconds. Add the tomatoes, stock
and salt and pepper to taste and cook for
10 minutes.

3 Add the chick-peas to the pan and
continue cooking for a further 5
minutes. Stir in the mint and cream and
reheat gently. Taste and adjust the
seasoning, if necessary. Serve hot with
plain or pilau rice, or with parathas, if
preferred.

STEP 1b

STEP 2

YOGURT

You could use natural yogurt instead of
cream in this dish, in which case first
blend it with ½ teaspoon cornflour
(cornstarch) before adding to the pan and
heating gently, stirring constantly. The
cornflour (cornstarch) helps stabilize the
yogurt to prevent it separating during
heating.

STEP 3

STEP 1

STEP 2

STEP 3

STEP 4

VEGETABLE CURRY

This colourful and interesting mixture of vegetables, cooked in a spicy sauce, is excellent served with pilau rice and naan bread. Vary the vegetables according to personal preferences.

SERVES 4

250 g/8 oz turnips or swede, peeled
1 aubergine (eggplant), leaf end trimmed
350 g/12 oz new potatoes, scrubbed
250 g/8 oz cauliflower
250 g/8 oz button mushrooms, wiped
1 large onion, peeled
250 g/8 oz carrots, peeled
6 tbsp vegetable ghee or oil
2 garlic cloves, peeled and crushed
5 cm/2 in ginger root, peeled and chopped
1-2 fresh green chillies, seeded and chopped
1 tbsp paprika
2 tsp ground coriander
1 tbsp mild or medium curry powder or paste
450 ml/³/₄ pint/1³/₄ cups vegetable stock
1 x 425 g/14 oz can chopped tomatoes
salt
1 green (bell) pepper, seeded and sliced
15 ml/1 tbsp cornflour (cornstarch)
150 ml/¹/₄ pint/²/₃ cup coconut milk
2-3 tbsp ground almonds
coriander sprigs, to garnish

1 Cut the turnips or swede, aubergine (eggplant) and potatoes into 1 cm (½ in) cubes. Divide the cauliflower into small florets. Leave the mushrooms whole, or slice thickly, if preferred. Slice the onion and carrots.

2 Heat the ghee or oil in a large saucepan, add the onion, turnip, potato and cauliflower and cook gently for 3 minutes, stirring frequently. Add the garlic, ginger, chilli and spices and cook for 1 minute, stirring.

3 Add the stock, tomatoes, aubergine (eggplant) and mushrooms and season with salt. Cover and simmer gently for about 30 minutes or until tender, stirring occasionally. Add the green (bell) pepper, cover and continue cooking for a further 5 minutes.

4 Smoothly blend the cornflour (cornstarch) with the coconut milk and stir into the mixture. Add the ground almonds and simmer for 2 minutes, stirring all the time. Taste and adjust the seasoning, if necessary. Serve hot, garnished with coriander sprigs.

GROUND ALMONDS

The ground almonds used in this dish not only help to thicken the sauce but also add richness and flavour to it. For a less fiery flavour, reduce or omit the amount of chilli used.

STEP 1

STEP 2

STEP 3

STEP 4

SPICED BASMATI PILAU

Omit the broccoli and mushrooms from this recipe if you require only a simple spiced pilau. The whole spices are not meant to be eaten and may be removed before serving, if wished.

SERVES 6

500 g/1 lb/2½ cups basmati rice
175 g/6 oz broccoli, trimmed
6 tbsp vegetable oil
2 large onions, peeled and chopped
250 g/8 oz mushrooms, wiped and sliced
2 garlic cloves, peeled and crushed
6 cardamom pods, split
6 whole cloves
8 black peppercorns
1 cinnamon stick or piece of cassia bark
1 tsp ground turmeric
1.25 litres/2 pints/5 cups boiling vegetable stock or water
salt and freshly ground black pepper
60 g/2 oz/⅓ cup seedless raisins
60 g/2 oz/½ cup unsalted pistachios, coarsely chopped

1 Place the rice in a sieve and wash well under cold running water until the water runs clear. Drain. Trim off most of the broccoli stalk and cut into small florets, then quarter the stalk lengthways and cut diagonally into 1 cm/½ in pieces.

2 Heat the oil in a large saucepan, add the onions and broccoli stalks and cook gently for 3 minutes, stirring frequently. Add the mushrooms, rice, garlic and spices and cook gently for 1 minute, stirring frequently until the rice is coated in spiced oil.

3 Add the boiling stock and season with salt and pepper. Stir in the broccoli florets and return the mixture to the boil. Cover, reduce the heat and cook gently for 15 minutes without uncovering.

4 Remove from the heat and leave to stand for 5 minutes without uncovering. Add the raisins and pistachios and gently fork through to fluff up the grains. Serve hot.

VARIATION

For added richness, you could stir a spoonful of vegetable ghee through the rice mixture just before serving. A little diced red pepper and a few cooked peas or sweetcorn kernels forked through at step 4 add a colourful touch.

CHAPTER THREE

Accompaniments

Bread accompanies nearly every meal in the form of parathas, which are basically fried chapattis; Naan, or leavened baked bread; crisp and crunchy poppadoms, flavoured or plain; and puris, small rounds of deep-fried bread that are sometimes stuffed with savoury ingredients.

Vegetable accompaniments come in all guises, as mixed curried dishes; as fritters, tasty with a spoonful of relish; and as bhajis, which are basically fried and spiced vegetables. They all contribute to give an Indian meal flavour and texture as well as extra nourishment.

Needless to say rice is a staple food and is served as a matter of course with virtually every meal. Experiment by cooking it in a little coconut milk with just a pinch of spices or garam masala to liven up plain boiled or steamed rice. Also consider serving spiced potatoes and cooked lentils as an alternative to rice – they make a welcome change and provide good nutrition.

Opposite: *A spice market in India.*

STEP 1

STEP 2a

STEP 2b

STEP 3

CURRIED OKRA

Okra, also known as bhindi and ladies' fingers, are a favourite Indian vegetable. They are now sold in many of the larger supermarkets, as well as Indian food stores and specialist greengrocers.

SERVES 4

500 g/ 1 lb fresh okra
4 tbsp vegetable ghee or oil
1 bunch spring onions (scallions), trimmed
*   and sliced*
2 garlic cloves, peeled and crushed
5 cm/ 2 in ginger root, peeled and chopped
1 tsp minced chilli (from a jar)
1½ tsp ground cumin
1 tsp ground coriander
1 tsp ground turmeric
1 x 250 g/8 oz can chopped tomatoes
150 ml/¼ pint/⅔ cup vegetable stock
salt and freshly ground black pepper
1 tsp garam masala
chopped fresh coriander, to garnish

1 Wash the okra, trim off the stalks and pat dry. Heat the ghee or oil in a large pan, add the spring onions (scallions), garlic, ginger and chilli and fry gently for 1 minute, stirring frequently.

2 Stir in the spices and fry gently for 30 seconds, then add the tomatoes, stock and okra. Season with salt and pepper to taste and simmer for about 15 minutes, stirring and turning the mixture occasionally. The okra should be cooked but still a little crisp.

3 Sprinkle with the garam masala, taste and adjust the seasoning, if necessary. Garnish with the chopped coriander and serve hot.

COOK'S TIP

If preferred, slice the okra into rings, add to the mixture (step 2), cover and cook until tender-crisp, stirring occasionally. When you buy fresh okra, make sure the pods are not shrivelled and that they do not have any brown spots. Once you get it home it will keep for 3 days tightly wrapped in the refrigerator.

AUBERGINE (EGGPLANT) IN SAFFRON

Here is a quick and simple, delicately spiced and delicious way to cook aubergines (eggplant).

STEP 1a

SERVES 4

a good pinch of saffron strands, finely
    crushed
1 tbsp boiling water
1 large aubergine (eggplant)
3 tbsp vegetable oil
1 large onion, peeled and coarsely chopped
2 garlic cloves, peeled and crushed
2.5 cm/1 in ginger root, peeled and chopped
1¹/₂ tbsp mild or medium curry paste
1 tsp cumin seeds
150 ml/¹/₄ pint/²/₃ cup double (heavy)
    cream
150 ml/¹/₄ pint/²/₃ cup strained Greek
    yogurt
2 tbsp mango chutney, chopped if necessary
salt and freshly ground black pepper

1 Place the saffron in a small bowl, add the boiling water and leave to infuse for 5 minutes. Trim the leaf end off the aubergine (eggplant), cut lengthways into quarters, then into 1 cm/½ in thick slices.

2 Heat the oil in a large frying pan, add the onion and cook gently for 3 minutes. Stir in the aubergine (eggplant), garlic, ginger, curry paste and cumin and cook gently for 3 minutes.

3 Stir in the saffron water, cream, yogurt and chutney and cook gently for 8-10 minutes, stirring frequently, until the aubergine (eggplant) is cooked through and tender. Season with salt and pepper to taste and serve hot.

STEP 1b

STEP 2

YOGURT

You will find that yogurt adds a creamy texture and pleasant tartness to this sauce. If you are worried about it curdling on heating, add a tablespoonful at a time and stir it in well before adding another. A little cornflour (cornstarch) blended with the yogurt before cooking, also helps prevent it from separating when heated.

STEP 3

STEP 1a

STEP 1b

STEP 2

STEP 3

SPINACH & CAULIFLOWER BHAJI

This excellent vegetable dish goes well with most Indian food – and it is simple and quick-cooking, too.

SERVES 4

1 cauliflower
500 g/1 lb fresh spinach, washed, or
    250 g/8 oz frozen spinach, defrosted
4 tbsp vegetable ghee or oil
2 large onions, peeled and coarsely chopped
2 garlic cloves, peeled and crushed
2.5 cm/1 in ginger root, peeled and chopped
1¼ tsp cayenne pepper, or to taste
1 tsp ground cumin
1 tsp ground turmeric
2 tsp ground coriander
1 x 425 g/14 oz can chopped tomatoes
300 ml/½ pint/1¼ cups vegetable stock
salt and freshly ground black pepper

1 Divide the cauliflower into small florets, discarding the hard central stalk. Trim the stalks from spinach leaves. Heat the ghee or oil in a large saucepan, add the onions and cauliflower florets and fry the vegetables gently for about 3 minutes, stirring frequently.

2 Add the garlic, ginger and spices and cook gently for 1 minute. Stir in the tomatoes and the stock and season with salt and pepper. Bring to the boil, cover, reduce the heat and simmer gently for 8 minutes.

3 Add the spinach to the pan, stirring and turning to wilt the leaves. Cover and simmer gently for about 8-10 minutes, stirring frequently until the spinach has wilted and the cauliflower is tender. Serve hot.

SPINACH

You may prefer to use frozen spinach in this recipe, in which case you require 250 g/8 oz frozen leaf spinach which must be defrosted and well drained before adding to the mixture and heating through.

FRIED SPICED POTATOES

Deliciously good and a super accompaniment to almost any main course dish, though rather high in calories!

SERVES 4-6

2 onions, peeled and quartered
5 cm/2 in ginger root, peeled and finely
    chopped
2 garlic cloves, peeled
2-3 tbsp mild or medium curry paste
4 tbsp water
750 g/1½ lb new potatoes
vegetable oil, for deep frying
3 tbsp vegetable ghee or oil
150 ml/¼ pint/⅔ cup strained Greek
    yogurt
150 ml/¼ pint/⅔ cup double (heavy)
    cream
3 tbsp chopped fresh mint
salt and freshly ground black pepper
½ bunch spring onions (scallions), trimmed
    and chopped, to garnish

1 Place the onions, ginger, garlic, curry paste and water in a blender or food processor and process until smooth, scraping down the sides of machine and blending again, if necessary.

2 Cut the potatoes into quarters – the pieces need to be about 2.5 cm/ 1 in in size – and pat dry with absorbent kitchen paper. Heat the oil in a deep-fat fryer to 180°C/350°F/Gas 4 and fry the

potatoes, in batches, for about 5 minutes or until golden brown, turning frequently. Remove from the pan and drain on paper towels.

3 Heat the ghee or oil in a large frying pan, add the curry and onion mixture and fry gently for 2 minutes, stirring all the time. Add the yogurt, cream and 2 tablespoons of mint and mix well.

4 Add the fried potatoes and stir until coated in the sauce. Cook for a further 5-7 minutes or until heated through and sauce has thickened, stirring frequently. Season with salt and pepper to taste and sprinkle with the remaining mint and sliced spring onions (scallions). Serve immediately.

STEP 1

STEP 2

STEP 3

STEP 5

MIXED (BELL) PEPPER POORIS

Wholemeal pooris are easy to make and so good to eat served with a topping of spicy mixed (bell) peppers and yogurt. You may, of course, simply make the pooris to serve plain with other dishes, if wished.

SERVES 6

POORIS:
125 g/4 oz/ 1 cup plain wholemeal flour
1 tbsp vegetable ghee or oil
2 good pinches of salt
75 ml/ 3 fl oz/¹/₃ cup hot water
vegetable oil, for shallow frying
natural yogurt, to serve
coriander sprigs, to garnish

TOPPING:
4 tbsp vegetable ghee or oil
1 large onion, peeled, quartered and thinly sliced
¹/₂ red (bell) pepper, seeded and thinly sliced
¹/₂ green (bell) pepper, seeded and thinly sliced
¹/₄ aubergine (eggplant), cut lengthways into 6 wedges and sliced thinly
1 garlic clove, peeled and crushed
2.5 cm/ 1 in ginger root, peeled and chopped
¹/₂-1 tsp minced chilli (from a jar)
2 tsp mild or medium curry paste
1 x 250 g/8 oz can chopped tomatoes
salt

1 To make the pooris, put the flour in a bowl with the ghee or oil and salt. Add hot water and mix to form a fairly soft dough. Knead gently, cover with a damp cloth and leave for 30 minutes.

2 Meanwhile, prepare the topping. Heat the ghee or oil in a large saucepan, add the onion, (bell) peppers, aubergine (eggplant), garlic, ginger, chilli and curry paste and fry gently for 5 minutes. Stir in the tomatoes and salt to taste and simmer gently, uncovered, for 5 minutes, stirring occasionally until the sauce thickens. Remove from the heat.

3 Knead the dough on a floured surface and divide into 6. Roll each one to a round about 15 cm/6 in in diameter. Cover each one as you finish rolling, to prevent drying out.

4 Heat about 1 cm/½ in oil in a large frying pan. Add a poori, one at a time, and fry for about 15 seconds on each side until puffed and golden, turning frequently. Drain on paper towels and keep warm while cooking the remainder in the same way.

5 Reheat the vegetable mixture. Place a poori on each serving plate and top with the vegetable mixture. Add a spoonful of yogurt to each one and garnish with coriander sprigs. Serve hot.

STEP 1

STEP 2

STEP 3

STEP 4

SWEET HOT CARROTS & BEANS

Take care not to overcook the vegetables in this tasty dish – they are definitely at their best served tender-crisp. Remember to discard the whole dried chillies before serving the dish.

SERVES 4

*500 g/1 lb young carrots, trimmed and
    peeled if necessary
250 g/8 oz French beans
1 bunch spring onions (scallions) trimmed
4 tbsp vegetable ghee or oil
1 tsp ground cumin
1 tsp ground coriander
3 cardamom pods, split and seeds removed
2 whole dried red chillies
2 garlic cloves, peeled and crushed
1-2 tsp clear honey, to taste
1 tsp lime or lemon juice
salt and freshly ground black pepper
60 g/2 oz/$^1/_2$ cup unsalted, toasted cashews
1 tbsp chopped fresh coriander or parsley
slices of lime or lemon and coriander sprigs,
    to garnish*

1 Cut the carrots lengthways into quarters and then in half crossways if very long. Top and tail the beans. Cut the spring onions into 5 cm/2 in pieces. Cook the carrots and beans in a saucepan containing a little boiling, salted water for 5-6 minutes according to how tender-crisp you like vegetables. Drain well.

2 Heat the ghee or oil in a large frying pan, add the spring onions (scallions), carrots, beans, cumin, coriander, cardamom seeds and whole dried chillies. Cook gently for 2 minutes, stirring frequently.

3 Stir in the garlic, honey and lemon or lime juice and continue cooking for a further 2 minutes, stirring occasionally. Season to taste with salt and pepper. Remove and discard the whole chillies.

4 Sprinkle the vegetables with the toasted cashews and chopped coriander, mix together lightly. Serve immediately, garnished with slices of lime or lemon and coriander sprigs.

CARROTS

If the carrots are very slender it may not be necessary to cut them into quarters, simply trim the leafy ends, scrub well and cook in the boiling, salted water for a minute or two before adding the French beans to ensure all the vegetables cook evenly.

POTATO FRITTERS WITH RELISH

These are incredibly simple to make and sure to be popular served as a tempting snack or as an accompaniment to almost any Indian main course dish.

STEP 1

MAKES 8

60 g/2 oz/¹/₂ cup plain wholemeal flour
¹/₂ tsp ground coriander
¹/₂ tsp cumin seeds
¹/₄ tsp chilli powder
¹/₂ tsp ground turmeric
¹/₄ tsp salt
1 egg
3 tbsp milk
350 g/12 oz potatoes, peeled
1-2 garlic cloves, peeled and crushed
4 spring onions (scallions), trimmed and
    chopped
60 g/2 oz sweetcorn kernels
vegetable oil for shallow frying

ONION AND TOMATO RELISH:

1 onion, peeled
250 g/8 oz tomatoes
2 tbsp chopped fresh coriander
2 tbsp chopped fresh mint
2 tbsp lemon juice
¹/₂ tsp roasted cumin seeds
¹/₄ tsp salt
a few pinches of cayenne pepper, to taste

1 First make the relish. Cut the onion and tomatoes into small dice and place in a bowl with the remaining ingredients. Mix together well and leave to stand for at least 15 minutes before

serving to allow time for the flavours to blend.

2 Place the flour in a bowl, stir in the spices and salt and make a well in the centre. Add the egg and milk and mix to form a fairly thick batter.

STEP 2

3 Coarsely grate the potatoes, place in a sieve and rinse well under cold running water. Drain and squeeze dry, then stir into the batter with the garlic, spring onions (scallions) and corn.

4 Heat about 5 mm/¼ in oil in a large frying pan and add a few tablespoonfuls of the mixture at a time, flattening each one to form a thin cake. Fry gently for 2-3 minutes or until golden brown and cooked through, turning frequently.

STEP 3

5 Drain on paper towels and keep hot while frying the remaining mixture in the same way. Serve hot with onion and tomato relish.

STEP 4

PARATHAS

These triangular shaped breads are so easy to make and are the perfect addition to most Indian meals. Serve hot, spread with a little butter, if wished.

STEP 1

MAKES 6

90 g/ 3 oz/ ³/₄ cup plain wholemeal flour
90 g/ 3 oz/ ³/₄ cup plain white flour
a good pinch of salt
1 tbsp vegetable oil, plus extra for greasing
75 ml/ 3 fl oz/ ¹/₃ cup tepid water

1 Place the flours and the salt in a bowl. Drizzle 1 tablespoon of oil over the flour, add the tepid water and mix to form a soft dough, adding a little more water, if necessary. Knead on a lightly floured surface until smooth, then cover and leave for 30 minutes.

2 Knead the dough on a floured surface and divide into 6 equal pieces. Shape each one into a ball. Roll out on a floured surface to a 15 cm/6 in round and brush very lightly with oil.

3 Fold in half, and then in half again to form a triangle. Roll out to form an 18 cm/7 in triangle (when measured from point to centre top), dusting with extra flour as necessary.

4 Brush a large frying pan with a little oil and heat until hot, then add one or two parathas and cook for about 1-1½ minutes. Brush the surfaces

STEP 2

very lightly with oil, then turn and cook the other sides for 1½ minutes until cooked through.

5 Place the cooked parathas on a plate and cover with foil, or place between a clean tea towel to keep warm, while cooking the remainder in the same way, greasing the pan between cooking each batch.

STEP 3

ALTERNATIVE

If the parathas puff up a lot during cooking, press down lightly with a fish slice. Make parathas in advance, if wished: wrap in kitchen foil and reheat in a hot oven for about 15 minutes when required.

STEP 4

CHAPTER FOUR

Desserts

The Indians frequently finish a meal with fresh fruit for dessert from the colourful supply available which includes mangoes, papayas, bananas, guavas and pears. Richer concoctions like carrot halva, mango ice-cream, ice cool sherbets and saffron-scented rice pudding are served only on special occasions such as a religious festival. In India they would be served on the very finest tableware and decorated with *varq*, the edible silver or gold leaf.

Indian rice pudding is a true classic, but is cooked in a saucepan over a low heat rather than baked in the oven. It is very sweet, often saffron or rose-water scented and sprinkled with chopped nuts like pistachios. It is perhaps one of the most popular of all desserts made in Indian households. Other favourites like ice-creams, coconut cream moulds and halva also make great use of milk.

Do try some of these dishes, for it is true to say that Indian restaurants offer little in the way of special Indian desserts and they are always a pleasant and enjoyable taste experience.

Opposite: *Pavilions on Lake Gadsi-Sar, Rajastan.*

STEP 1

STEP 2

STEP 3

STEP 4

MANGO ICE-CREAM

This delicious ice-cream with its refreshing tang of mango and lime makes the perfect ending to a hot and spicy meal. You will find canned mango slices are widely available from larger supermarkets.

SERVES 4-6

150 ml/¹/₄ pint/²/₃ cup single cream
2 egg yolks
¹/₂ tsp cornflour (cornstarch)
1 tsp water
2 x 439 g/14 oz cans mango slices in syrup, drained
1 tbsp lime or lemon juice
150 ml/¹/₄ pint/²/₃ cup double (heavy) cream
mint sprigs, to decorate

1 Heat the single cream in a saucepan until hot (but do not allow it to boil). Place the egg yolks in a bowl with the cornflour (cornstarch) and water and mix together until smooth. Pour the hot cream on to the egg yolk mixture, stirring all the time.

2 Return the mixture to the pan and place over a very low heat, whisking or stirring all the time until the mixture thickens and coats the back of a wooden spoon. (Do not try and hurry this process or the mixture will overcook and spoil.) Pour into a bowl.

3 Purée the drained mango slices in a blender or food processor until smooth. Mix with the custard and stir in

the lime juice. Whip the double (heavy) cream until softly peaking and fold into the mango mixture until thoroughly combined.

4 Transfer the mixture to a loaf tin or shallow freezerproof container. Cover and freeze for 2-3 hours or until half-frozen and still mushy in the centre. Turn the mixture into a bowl and mash well with a fork until smooth. Return to the container, cover and freeze again until firm.

5 Transfer the container of ice cream to the main compartment of the refrigerator for about 30 minutes before serving to allow it to soften slightly. Scoop or spoon the ice cream into serving dishes and decorate with mint sprigs.

ALTERNATIVE

Use the drained mango syrup for adding to fruit salads or for mixing into drinks.

SAFFRON-SPICED RICE PUDDING

This rich and comforting pudding is first cooked in milk delicately flavoured with saffron and cinnamon. Raisins, dried apricots, almonds and cream are then added to the mixture before baking.

STEP 1

SERVES 4-5
OVEN: 160°C / 325°F / GAS 3

600 ml / 1 pint / 2½ cups creamy milk
several pinches of saffron strands, finely crushed (see below)
60 g / 2 oz / ¼ cup short-grain (pudding) rice
1 cinnamon stick or piece of cassia bark
45 g / 1½ oz granulated sugar
30 g / 1 oz / ¼ cup seedless raisins or sultanas
30 g / 1 oz / ¼ cup ready-soaked dried apricots, chopped
1 egg, beaten
75 ml / 3 fl oz / ⅓ cup single cream
15 g / ½ oz / 1 tbsp butter, diced
15 g / ½ oz / 2 tbsp flaked almonds
freshly grated nutmeg, for sprinkling
cream, for serving (optional)

1 Place the milk and crushed saffron in a non-stick saucepan and bring to the boil. Stir in the rice and cinnamon stick, reduce the heat and simmer very gently, uncovered, for 25 minutes, stirring frequently until tender.

2 Remove the pan from the heat and discard the cinnamon stick from the rice mixture. Stir in the sugar, raisins and apricots, then beat in the egg, cream and diced butter.

3 Transfer the mixture to a greased ovenproof pie or flan dish, sprinkle with the almonds and freshly grated nutmeg, to taste. Cook in the preheated oven for 25-30 minutes until mixture is set and lightly golden. Serve hot with extra cream, if wished.

STEP 2a

STEP 2b

SAFFRON

For a slightly stronger saffron flavour, place the saffron strands on a small piece of kitchen foil and toast them lightly under a hot grill for a few moments (take care not to overcook them or the flavour will spoil) and crush finely between fingers and thumb before adding to the milk.

STEP 3

STEP 1

STEP 2

STEP 3A

STEP 3B

COCONUT CREAM MOULDS

Smooth, creamy and refreshing – these tempting little custards are made with an unusual combination of coconut milk, cream and eggs.

SERVES 8
OVEN: 140°C/275°F/GAS1

CARAMEL:
125 g/4 oz/¹/₂ cup granulated sugar
150 ml/¹/₄ pint/ 2/3 cup water

CUSTARD:
300 ml/¹/₂ pint/ 1¹/₄ cups water
90g/ 3 oz creamed coconut, chopped
2 eggs
2 egg yolks
1¹/₂ tbsp caster sugar
300 ml/¹/₂ pint/ 1¹/₄ cups single cream
sliced banana or slivers of fresh pineapple
1-2 tbsp freshly grated or desiccated
(shredded) coconut

1 Have ready 8 small ovenproof dishes about 150 ml/¼ pint/⅔ cup capacity. To make the caramel, place the sugar and water in a saucepan and heat gently to dissolve the sugar, then boil rapidly, without stirring, until the mixture turns a rich golden brown.

2 Remove at once from the heat and dip the base of the pan into a basin of cold water (this stops it cooking). Quickly but carefully pour the caramel into the ovenproof dishes to coat the bases.

3 To make the custard, place the water in the same saucepan, add the coconut and heat until coconut dissolves, stirring all the time. Place the eggs, egg yolks and caster sugar in a bowl and beat well with a fork. Add the hot coconut milk and stir well to dissolve the sugar. Stir in the cream and strain mixture into a jug.

4 Arrange the dishes in a roasting tin and fill with enough cold water to come halfway up the sides of the dishes. Pour the custard mixture into the caramel-lined dishes, cover with greaseproof paper or foil and cook in the oven for about 40 minutes or until set.

5 Remove the dishes from the roasting tin and leave to cool. Chill overnight in the refrigerator. To serve, run a knife around the edge of each dish and turn out on to a serving plate. Serve with slices of banana or slivers of fresh pineapple sprinkled with freshly grated or desiccated coconut.

SWEET CARROT HALVA

This nutritious dessert, made from grated carrots simmered in milk, is flavoured with spices, nuts and raisins. It is delicious served plain or with thick cream or yogurt.

SERVES 6

750 g/ 1¹/₂ lb carrots, peeled and grated
750 ml/ 1¹/₄ pints/ 3 cups milk
1 cinnamon stick or piece of cassia bark
  (optional)
4 tbsp vegetable ghee or oil
60 g/ 2 oz/¹/₄ cup granulated sugar
30 g/ 1 oz/¹/₄ cup unsalted pistachio nuts,
  chopped
30-50 g/ 1-2 oz/¹/₄-¹/₂ cup blanched
  almonds, slivered or chopped
60 g/ 2 oz/¹/₃ cup seedless raisins
8 cardamom pods, split and seeds removed
  and crushed
thick cream or yogurt, to serve

1 Put the grated carrots, milk and cinnamon or cassia, if using, into a large, heavy-based saucepan and bring to the boil. Reduce the heat to a simmer and cook, uncovered, for 35-40 minutes, or until the mixture is thick (with no milk remaining). Stir the mixture frequently during cooking to prevent it sticking.

2 Discard the cinnamon. Heat the ghee or oil in a non-stick frying pan, add the carrot mixture and stir-fry over a medium heat for about 5 minutes or until the carrots take on a glossy sheen.

3 Add the sugar, pistachios, almonds, raisins and crushed cardamom seeds, mix well and continue frying for a further 3-4 minutes, stirring frequently. Serve warm or cold with thick cream or yogurt.

GRATING

The quickest and easiest way to grate this quantity of carrots is by using a food processor fitted with the appropriate blade. This mixture may be prepared ahead of time and reheated in the microwave when required. Use green cardamoms as these have the best flavour.

INDIAN VEGETARIAN COOKING

TASTY ACCOMPANIMENTS

Here is a selection of deliciously easy accompaniments to complement your Indian dishes.

Apple and onion relish peel, core and coarsely grate 1 large cooking apple into a bowl. Add ½ bunch chopped spring onions, 2 tsp vinegar or lemon juice, 1-2 tsp caster sugar, to taste, and ½ tsp roasted cumin seeds. Mix well and chill before serving, sprinkled with chopped fresh coriander.

Radish and cucumber yogurt put 600 ml / 1 pint/2½ cups natural yogurt into a bowl and season with salt and freshly ground black pepper. Stir in ½ bunch trimmed and coarsely chopped radishes, ¼ unpeeled, diced cucumber, 1 small chopped onion and 15-30 ml/ 1-2 tbsp chopped fresh mint. Serve chilled.

Cucumber raita mix 600 ml / 1 pint/2½ cups natural yogurt with ¼ peeled and grated cucumber. Season with salt, freshly ground black pepper and a pinch or two of cayenne pepper. Just before serving, dry roast 1 tsp cumin seeds, then crush coarsely and sprinkle over the yogurt mixture just before serving. Add a little finely chopped fresh mint to the mixture, if wished.

continued opposite

Here is a mouthwatering collection of easy Indian-style vegetarian recipes ranging from mild and fragrant, to hot and fiery, or simply nice and spicy. So whether you are looking for a simple nutritious snack, a substantial family meal or a special dish for entertaining, this book has a recipe to suit most palates and all occasions. You will find all the ingredients used here are available from larger supermarkets.

SPICES

It is well worth investing in some spices, to give authentic flavour to your Indian cooking. Here are just a few suggestions to help give variety and interest to all manner of dishes – from soups and starters to main courses, accompaniments and desserts.

Cardamom small pods containing tiny black seeds with an aromatic flavour – green cardamoms are considered the best. These pods can be used whole or split (to fully appreciate the flavour from the seeds), or crushed and the seeds removed and used whole or ground, according to recipe requirements. The whole or split pods are not meant to be eaten and should be left on the side of the plate.

Cayenne pepper orange-red in colour, this ground pepper is extremely hot and pungent being made from dried red chillies. Not to be confused with paprika, which, although similar in colour, is mild-flavoured. Use caution with cayenne – a little goes a long way!

Chilli powder available in varying degrees of strength. Pure chilli powder is extremely hot and should be used sparingly. It is best to check the label on jars before buying as many powders are a blend of chilli and other spices and flavourings, and 'chilli seasoning' – a popular blend of spices – is quite mild.

Cinnamon made from the dried bark of a tropical tree is available in small sticks or ground. It is deliciously fragrant and used to great effect in both savoury and sweet dishes. The sticks are not edible and may be removed before serving, or used as a garnish or decoration.

Cassia comes from the bark of the cassia tree and is not as attractive and uniform in shape as cinnamon, although the flavour is good, being stronger and less delicate than cinnamon.

Cloves these dried unopened flower buds should be used with care as they are rather pungent in flavour and can become overpowering if used in quantity. Whole cloves are decorative but not meant to be eaten and may be removed before serving.

Coriander is available in seed or ground form and has a mild, spicy flavour with a slight orange peel fragrance. It is an essential spice in curry dishes.

Cumin available as seeds or ground. Cumin has a warm, pungent, aromatic flavour and is used extensively in Indian cooking.

Garam Masala is a ground aromatic mixture of spices that usually includes cardamom, cinnamon, cumin, cloves, peppercorns and nutmeg. It is used during and towards the end of cooking, or is sprinkled over dishes just before serving as an aromatic garnish. This spice mix is available ready-mixed, or you can make your own: finely grind together 1 tsp each black peppercorns and cumin seeds with 15ml/1 tsp cardamom seeds, 8 whole cloves, a 5 cm/2 inch cinnamon stick or piece of cassia bark and about ¼ freshly grated nutmeg. Store in an airtight container and use within 3 weeks.

Ginger fresh root ginger looks like a knobbly stem and should be peeled before being chopped or grated before use. Fresh ginger has a refreshing, pungent flavour and is an essential ingredient in many Indian dishes. Also available ready minced in jars.

Nutmeg available as whole nutmegs or ground – best to buy them whole and grate them yourself to fully appreciate the warm, sweet and aromatic flavour.

Paprika this bright red powder comes from a variety of red pepper and is frequently used in cooking to add colour to dishes. Although similar in colour to cayenne pepper, paprika has a mild flavour and is used in far greater quantity than cayenne.

Peppercorns are available in three colours – as white (ripe berries), black (unripened berries dried until dark greenish black in colour) and green (unripe berries). It is the black peppercorns with their warm, aromatic flavour that are most frequently used in Indian cooking. The peppercorns are used whole (in dishes such as biryani,when they are not meant to be eaten and should be left on the side of the plate) or they may be ground, in which case they should be freshly milled as required for once ground they quickly lose flavour.

Saffron comes from the stigmas of a species of crocus. It gives a distinctive flavour and rich yellow colouring to dishes. Saffron is available in small packets or jars – powdered or in strands – the strands have a better flavour.

Turmeric is an aromatic root, closely related to ginger, which is dried and ground to produce a bright orange-yellow powder. It has a warm, distinctive smell and delicate, earthy flavour and helps give dishes an attractive yellow colouring, but should not be used instead of saffron. Turmeric should be used with care as it can stain.

COOK'S SPICE NOTES

For the best flavour, buy the whole spices and grind them as and when required,

Tasty Accompaniments continued.

Carrot, raisin and onion salad coarsely grate 250g/8 oz carrots into a bowl. Peel and quarter 1 onion, cut into paper-thin slices and add to the carrots. Stir in 45 ml/3 tbsp seedless raisins and 15 ml/1 tbsp lemon juice. Season with ¼ tsp paprika, ½ tsp grated fresh ginger, salt and freshly ground black pepper. If wished, add slivers of fresh chilli (or a little minced chilli, from a jar) for a more fiery flavour. Mix all the ingredients well together and leave to stand for 30 minutes before serving, to allow time for the flavours to develop. Serve at room temperature or chilled.

DRINKS

When serving spicy dishes be sure to have a supply of refreshing drinks to hand – chilled mineral water, iced water or fruit juice are excellent choices. For special occasions and for a deliciously refreshing drink to sip during a hot, spicy meal, serve iced water flavoured with spices, such as cardamom, cumin, cassia or cinnamon. Wine is not good served with Indian foods, since the taste is overpowered by the strong flavours of the food, so opt instead for chilled lagers and light beers. You could also provide a jug of Lassi – a delicious and nutritious Indian drink of lightly spiced yogurt which is designed to cool the palate.

To MAKE LASSI: put 600 ml/1 pint/2½ cups natural yogurt in a blender or food processor with 1.5 litres/2½ pints/6¼ cups cold water, 1-2 tsp lemon juice, 15 ml/1 tbsp chopped fresh mint, ½ tsp each salt and dry-roasted cumin and freshly ground black pepper to taste. Blend for about 1 minute, then serve in a jug or tall glasses filled with crushed ice.

To MAKE SWEET LASSI: omit the lemon juice, mint, salt, cumin and pepper and instead flavour the yogurt and water with sugar, ground cardamom and a little rosewater, to taste. Blend as above and serve over crushed ice.

using a pestle and mortar or rolling pin, for small quantities, and a small electric mill or coffee grinder, for larger amounts. Whole spices keep their flavour and aroma far longer than ready-ground spices.

If you prefer to make the most of the ready-ground spices then buy in small quantities and store them in a cool, dry, dark place in airtight jars and remember that once opened the spices begin to lose flavour and aroma. Roasting or dry-frying spices is a technique applied in Indian cooking which brings out a certain flavour and roasted aroma from spices and, at the same time makes them easier to crush. Use a heavy-based frying pan and fry the whole spices in a dry pan (without oil or liquid) over a moderate heat, shaking the pan and stirring the spices until they turn a shade darker (take care not to overheat or the flavour of the spices becomes bitter). As soon as you smell the roasted aroma from spices tip them at once onto a plate. Cool and use as required.

STORECUPBOARD STANDBYS

We are almost spoilt for choice with the excellent range of commercially prepared products now available in supermarkets. So, when time is at a premium, make the most of these 'convenience' items. Spice mixes such as curry powders, garam masala and tandoori spices, plus the ready-made curry pastes, sauces and jars of ready-minced chilli and fresh ginger are invaluable for making quick and authentic-tasting Indian dishes. There is also a wonderful selection of

accompaniments available to include with your homemade dishes – delicious items like poppadums, naan bread, chapatis, parathas, samosas and onion bhajis, plus a tempting range of Indian pickles and chutneys to choose from.

Coriander (herb) Fresh coriander is a favourite herb in Indian cooking. The green leaves (rather similar in appearance to flat-leaved parsley) are used extensively in dishes for flavouring and as a garnish. It is now widely available in supermarkets and specialist green grocers, but if you have difficulty buying coriander, use fresh flat-leaf parsley as a substitute.

Chillies Fresh chillies vary in hotness according to variety. Remember that the seeds are the hottest part, so it is up to you whether you include some or not. Always handle chillies with caution, preferably wearing rubber gloves as the juices are extremely pungent. Wash hands, utensils, board or work surface thoroughly after preparing and handling chillies and do not get your fingers near your eyes as this can be very painful. For convenience, make use of the ready-minced chilli available in jars.

Ghee Indian cooks sometimes like to use ghee, or clarified butter, for cooking. It gives a deliciously rich, nutty flavour to dishes and a glossy sheen to curried sauces and can be cooked at high temperatures without burning. However, vegetable oil may be used in any of the recipes here, in place of the ghee, if preferred. Ghee can be bought from many of the larger supermarkets and Asian grocers. It is worth noting that ghee is not suitable for vegans, although there is a vegetarian ghee available from many supermarkets and health food shops. To make your own ghee: melt unsalted butter in a saucepan and simmer gently for about 20 minutes until it becomes clear and a whitish residue settles at the bottom of the mixture. Remove the pan from the heat and skim off any scum from the surface. Leave the mixture to cool, then strain off the clear liquid and use as required. It will keep for up to 3 months stored in a container in the refrigerator.

Coconut Coconut is used extensively in Indian cooking to add flavour and creaminess to various dishes and sauces (both savoury and sweet). The best flavour comes from freshly grated coconut, although ready-prepared desiccated coconut makes an excellent standby.

Fresh grated coconut freezes successfully, so is well worth preparing when you've time to spare. Break the coconut in half, drain off the liquid and remove the flesh from its shell. Using a potato peeler, remove the brown skin, break the flesh into pieces and process in a food processor until finely grated. You can, if preferred, grate larger pieces on a cheese grater. Pack in small usable quantities and freeze for up to 3 months. Thaw and use as required.

Coconut milk and creamed coconut are two popular ingredients in Indian cooking – the milk is available in cans, or as coconut milk powder in sachets; and creamed coconut comes in 198-225 g/ 7-8 oz packets. To make your own coconut milk, chop a packet of creamed coconut and place in a jug. Add enough boiling water to come to the 600 ml/1pint/2½ cups mark and stir to dissolve. Cool and use as required.

Yogurt Yogurt plays an important part in vegetarian Indian cooking for it is used not only as a creamy flavouring in numerous dishes and sauces, but also as an accompaniment to hot dishes. Strained Greek yogurt, with its tart, creamy flavour, is the one that most closely resembles the homemade yogurt (dahi) made in the majority of Indian homes, though any natural yogurt may be used. If the yogurt is thick, stir or whisk it for a few seconds to thin the consistency before using. Yogurt is frequently stirred into dishes towards the end of cooking and can become curdled if overheated. To prevent this happening, blend the yogurt with a little cornflour (cornstarch) before heating – you require ½ tsp to every 150 ml/¼ pint yogurt – this helps stabilize the mixture and prevents it separating when cooked. Alternatively, add the yogurt to the cooked mixture, a spoonful at a time, stirring well to incorporate it into the mixture before adding the next spoonful.

Rice Long-grain rice (also called American long-grain or Patna rice) is the most widely available and the cheapest, although basmati rice with its slender grains and fine aromatic flavour is the best variety to use for Indian savoury

ROASTED SPICE MIX

This is a very handy mixture to keep in your storecupboard. The roasted, ground mixture can be kept in an airtight container. Add 1 teaspoonful when cooking rice, curries, dals or stews to give a quick and easy Indian flavour to your dishes.

4 tbsp coriander seeds
1 tbsp cumin seeds

1. Heat a small frying pan over a medium heat. When hot, add the seeds and toast over the heat until they turn a few shades darker.

2. Remove the pan from the heat and let the seeds cool slightly.

3. Place the seeds in a coffee grinder and grind as finely as possible. Alternatively, grind the seeds in a pestle and mortar. Store in an airtight container.

DAL

Dal are actually split peas, lentils and beans. There are several different kinds available, which can all be used to make the Dal that you will find on the menu in Indian restaurants.

250 g/8 oz chana dal or yellow
  split peas, soaked
1.25 litres/2 pints water
1/2 tsp turmeric
1 onion, chopped
1 tsp ground cumin
2 tbsp vegetable oil
1/2 tsp mustard seeds
2 garlic cloves, crushed
2 dried chillies, seeded and
  chopped
250 g/8 oz canned chopped
  tomatoes
salt and pepper

1. Drain and rinse the lentils then place in a pan with the water and turmeric. Bring to the boil then cover and simmer for 30 minutes.

2. Add the onion and cumin, stir, cover and cook for another 15 minutes.

3. Meanwhile, heat the oil in a small pan and add the mustard seeds. When the seeds pop add the chillies and tomatoes. Cook for 2-3 minutes then add the contents of the pan to the lentils. Stir well, add salt and pepper to taste and serve.

dishes whenever possible. Basmati rice is rather more expensive, so save it for special occasions if you cannot afford to use it every time. There are many varieties of rice on the market, as well as numerous packets of easy-cook, pre-cooked and pre-fluffed types, which makes it almost impossible to give exact cooking times, so if unsure, the best advice is to follow the packet instructions to ensure good results. Rice (especially basmati) should be rinsed in a sieve under cold running water before cooking to rid it of the starchy residue left from the milling process. Brown rice is the whole unpolished grain with only the tough outer husk removed. It has a nutty flavour and chewy texture and therefore contains larger amounts of vitamins, minerals and protein than the white polished rice. It takes longer to cook than white rice, generally around 40 minutes. It may be used in any recipes which call for long-grain rice, but if the dish is cooked by the absorption method (such as a biryani), you will need to allow extra liquid and a longer cooking time.

Pulses (dal) Dried beans, peas and lentils are an essential ingredient in the vegetarian diet helping provide a large portion of the daily protein requirement – and Indian cooking is renowned for its interesting and delicious range of pulse dishes. However, although these pulses (known collectively as Dal) are rich in protein, they are not a complete protein in themselves and need to be served with either a grain (such as rice) and/or a bread (naan, chapatis, pooris or parathas), plus a dairy product like

yogurt or cheese.

Dried pulses come in a range of colours and shapes (round, oval, kidney-shaped or capsule-like). They may be large, medium or small, whole or split (the splitting helps them cook much faster) and are sometimes skinned. There is a wide range of pulses available from supermarkets, health food shops and Asian stores. It is important to check pulses before cooking as the packets may contain small stones and husks which should be removed before using.

Whole dried pulses (with the exception of lentils) should be soaked overnight in cold water before cooking, or prepared by the quick-soak method: place the pulse in a saucepan, cover with cold water and bring to the boil, then boil rapidly for 10 minutes. Remove the pan from the heat, cover and leave the beans to soak in the water for 3 hours. Once the pulses have been soaked (by the slow or quick method), they should be drained, placed in a pan with fresh cold water to cover and boiled rapidly for 10 minutes to destroy the toxins present in some beans. The heat is then reduced and the beans simmered for the required time given in a recipe. Cooking times vary according to the type of pulse and its freshness.

Dried pulses keep for up to 6 months, after which time the skins begin to toughen, so it's best to buy them from a supermarket with a quick turnover to ensure you are getting fresh stock. Store the pulses in an airtight container. When seasoning pulses, add salt towards the end of cooking, never at the beginning as this tends to toughen the skins. For extra flavour add one or two garlic cloves or bay leaves, or an onion studded with cloves to the pan when boiling the pulses.

Here is a list of the more widely used pulses – all available from supermarkets.

Split red lentils bright, shiny orangey-red lentils with a pleasant, mild flavour. This type does not require soaking before cooking, and once cooked, breaks down to become soft and pulpy in texture. Used in many dishes, including soups, curries and sauces to thicken them and to add protein.

Continental lentils these greenish-brown lentils are larger and have a stronger flavour than the split red type. They retain their shape after cooking, although may be cooked for longer and mashed to a pulpy texture, if wished. This type are sometimes soaked for a time before cooking, or according to recipe instructions and are used in all manner of dishes such as vegetable koftas, soups, curried vegetable dishes and biryanis.

Chana dal although similar in appearance to yellow split peas, chana dal is the husked split, black chick pea, popular with vegetarians because of its high protein content. It is not as widely available as other dals, although you will find it in some of the larger supermarkets, as well as Indian grocers and health food shops. The recipes in this book use yellow split peas instead of chana dal, but the latter may be used instead, if wished.

Chick peas these large, beige-coloured peas are shaped rather like hazelnuts and once cooked have a nutty flavour and slightly crunchy texture. Chick peas are also ground to make gram (or besan flour) – a fine yellow flour that is used in a variety of dishes, including pakoras and onion bhajis. Chick peas are also available ready-cooked in cans.

Black-eye beans these oval-shaped beans are greyish or beige in colour with a dark dot in the centre. They have a slightly smoky flavour and are excellent cooked in many dishes. Canned, ready-cooked black-eye beans are also available.

Red kidney beans these large, deep red, kidney-shaped beans have a slightly nutty flavour and are excellent cooked in spicy sauces, soups and all manner of vegetable dishes. Also available ready-cooked in cans.

Canned pulses Canned black-eye beans, red kidney beans and chick peas are a convenient and quick alternative to the dried variety and are widely available in supermarkets. These pulses are cooked and ready to eat, but before using, empty them into a sieve to drain and rinse under cold running water before using as required. You will see that the recipes in this book use only the canned beans and chick peas in order to cut out the lengthy cooking times otherwise involved, but the dried types may be used instead, if preferred, and the method of cooking, and the cooking times, adjusted accordingly. As the canned beans and peas tend to be quite soft in texture, they are more usually added to the various dishes towards the end of cooking time to prevent them becoming over-mushy.

BASMATI RICE

This is a foolproof way of cooking rice by the absorption method. Do not be tempted to lift the lid before the time is up, or the steam will escape and the rice will not be cooked.

250 g/8 oz basmati rice

1. Rinse the rice in several changes of water and drain thoroughly.

2. Place the rice in a heavy pan and add enough water so that the water level is 2.5 cm/1 inch above the level of the rice.

3. Bring the rice to a vigorous boil, then stir well. Cover the pan tightly and turn off the heat. Leave the pan on the stove for 25 minutes, then lift off the stove and leave, still covered, for another 10 minutes. Fork up the rice and serve.

INDEX

Accompaniments, 47-63, 74-5
almonds: vegetable curry, 42
apple and onion relish, 74
apricots: brown rice with fruit and nuts, 24
aubergines (eggplant): aubergine in saffron, 51
 chick peas and aubergine, 41
 spinach and aubergine, 36
 stuffed aubergines, 31

Basmati rice, 79
beans: Indian bean soup, 8
 jacket potatoes with, 34
bell pepper pooris, 56
besan flour, 16
bhaji, spinach and cauliflower, 52
biryani, lentil and vegetable, 32
black-eye beans, 79
 Indian bean soup, 8
 jacket potatoes with, 34
bread: parathas, 63
broccoli: spiced basmati pilau, 44

Canned pulses, 79
caramel: coconut cream moulds, 70
cardamom, 74
carrots: carrot, raisin and onion salad, 75
 grating, 73
 spicy dal and carrot soup, 12
 sweet carrot halva, 73
 sweet hot carrots and beans, 58
cashews: vegetable and cashew samosas, 19
 vegetable, nut and lentil koftas, 38
cassia, 74
cauliflower and spinach bhaji, 52
cayenne pepper, 74
chana dal, 28, 79
 dal, 78
cheese: muttar paneer, 27
chick-peas, 79
 chick-peas and aubergine (eggplant), 41
chilli powder, 74
chillies, 76
cinnamon, 74
cloves, 74
coconut, 77
 coconut cream moulds, 70
coconut milk, 77
coriander, 74-5, 76
corn and nut mix, spiced, 14
cucumber: cucumber raita, 74

 radish and cucumber yogurt, 74
cumin, 75
curries: curried okra, 48
 egg and lentil curry, 22
 vegetable curry, 42
custards: coconut cream moulds, 70

Dal, 78-9
 spicy dal and carrot soup, 12
dressing, yogurt, 38
drinks, 76

Eggplant (aubergines):
 eggplant in saffron, 51
 chick-peas and eggplant, 41
 spinach and eggplant, 36
 stuffed eggplant, 31
eggs, 22
 egg and lentil curry, 22

French beans: sweet hot carrots and beans, 58
fritters, potato, 61

Garam masala, 75
garlicky mushroom pakoras, 16
ghee, 76-7
ginger, 75
gram flour, 16

Halva, sweet carrot, 73

Ice-cream, mango, 66
Indian bean soup, 8
ingredients, 74-9

Koftas, vegetable, nut and lentil, 38

Lassi, 76
lentils, 79
 egg and lentil curry, 22
 lentil and vegetable biryani, 32
 spicy dal and carrot soup, 12
 stuffed aubergines (eggplant), 31
 vegetable, nut and lentil koftas, 38

Mango ice-cream, 66
milk: saffron-spiced rice pudding, 69
 sweet carrot halva, 73
minted pea & yogurt soup, 11
mushrooms: garlicky mushroom pakoras, 16
 spiced basmati pilau, 44
muttar paneer, 27

Nutmeg, 75
nuts: brown rice with fruit and nuts, 24
 spiced corn and nut mix, 14

Okra, curried, 48
onions: apple and onion relish, 74
 carrot, raisin and onion salad, 75
 onion and tomato relish, 61

Pakoras, garlicky mushroom, 16
paneer, muttar, 27
paprika, 75
parathas, 63
peas: minted pea & yogurt soup, 11
 muttar paneer, 27
peppercorns, 75
peppers (bell): mixed pepper pooris, 56
pilau, spiced basmati, 44
pooris, mixed (bell) pepper, 56
potatoes: fried spiced, 55
 jacket potatoes with beans, 34
 potato fritters with relish, 61
pulses, 78-9

Radish and cucumber yogurt, 74
raisins: carrot, raisin and onion salad, 75
raita, cucumber, 74
red kidney beans, 79
 jacket potatoes with, 34
relishes: apple and onion, 74
 onion and tomato, 61
rice, 77-8
 basmati rice, 79
 brown rice with fruit and nuts, 24
 lentil and vegetable biryani, 32
 saffron-spiced rice pudding, 69
 spiced basmati pilau, 44
roasted spice mix, 77

Saffron, 75
 aubergine (eggplant) in, 51
 saffron-spiced rice pudding, 69
salad, carrot, raisin and onion, 75
samosas, vegetable and cashew, 19
soups, 7-12
 Indian bean, 8
 minted pea & yogurt, 11
 spicy dal and carrot, 12
spices, 74-5
 roasted spice mix, 77
spinach: spinach and aubergine (eggplant), 36
 spinach and cauliflower bhaji, 52

split peas with vegetables, 28

Tomatoes: dal, 78
 muttar paneer, 27
 onion and tomato relish, 61
turmeric, 75

Vegetables: lentil and vegetable biryani, 32
 split peas with, 28
 vegetable and cashew samosas, 19
 vegetable curry, 42
 vegetable, nut and lentil koftas, 38
 see also onions; potatoes etc.

Yogurt, 77
 aubergine (eggplant) in saffron, 51
 chick-peas and aubergine (eggplant), 41
 cucumber raita, 74
 lassi, 76
 minted pea & yogurt soup, 11
 radish and cucumber yogurt, 74
 yogurt dressing, 38